Dog Breeds

English Springer Spaniels

BY LIBBY WILSON

WWW.APEXEDITIONS.COM

Copyright © 2025 by Apex Editions, Mendota Heights, MN 55120. All rights reserved. No part of this book may be reproduced or utilized in any form or by any means without written permission from the publisher.

Apex is distributed by North Star Editions:
sales@northstareditions.com | 888-417-0195

Produced for Apex by Red Line Editorial.

Photographs ©: iStockphoto, cover, 6–7, 18–19, 21, 22–23, 26, 29; Shutterstock Images, 1, 9, 10–11, 12, 14–15, 16–17, 20, 24–25, 27; Gareth Fuller/EMPPL PA Wire/AP Images, 4–5, 8; Farlap/Alamy, 13

Library of Congress Control Number: 2023921789

ISBN
978-1-63738-907-2 (hardcover)
978-1-63738-947-8 (paperback)
979-8-89250-044-9 (ebook pdf)
979-8-89250-005-0 (hosted ebook)

Printed in the United States of America
Mankato, MN
082024

NOTE TO PARENTS AND EDUCATORS

Apex books are designed to build literacy skills in striving readers. Exciting, high-interest content attracts and holds readers' attention. The text is carefully leveled to allow students to achieve success quickly. Additional features, such as bolded glossary words for difficult terms, help build comprehension.

TABLE OF CONTENTS

CHAPTER 1
FRIENDLY K9   4

CHAPTER 2
BREED HISTORY   10

CHAPTER 3
A SPRINGER'S LOOKS   16

CHAPTER 4
FAMILY DOGS   22

COMPREHENSION QUESTIONS • 28
GLOSSARY • 30
TO LEARN MORE • 31
ABOUT THE AUTHOR • 31
INDEX • 32

CHAPTER 1

FRIENDLY K9

An English springer spaniel hops into a police car. Her name is Mindy. She works with Officer Sutton. They are going on patrol.

Each police dog is paired with one officer. That person is called the dog's handler.

Many English springer spaniels are very friendly.

They spot a lost boy. He is crying. Mindy licks his hand. Petting Mindy calms the boy. Then Officer Sutton finds the boy's family.

FAST FACT

Police dogs are often called K9s. The word canine means "dog."

Sniffer dogs may be trained to point, sit, or bark when they find something.

Next, Mindy searches a house for **illegal** drugs. She sniffs every room. Mindy barks and scratches a wall. The police find drugs hidden inside.

SNIFFER DOGS

English springer spaniels have strong noses. They often work as sniffer dogs. They train to find weapons or drugs. They get toys as a **reward**.

Some sniffer dogs search for bombs. They may work at airports or other places with lots of people.

CHAPTER 2

BREED HISTORY

People in Europe have raised spaniels for hundreds of years. The dogs helped hunters find birds in fields. They **retrieved** what the hunters shot.

English springer spaniels often help people hunt pheasants.

Hunters often use dogs to run through fields and scare birds hiding in the grass.

In the 1800s, people began separating spaniels by type. One type got birds to fly up into the air. These dogs were called springers. By the 1900s, they were a unique **breed**.

SORTING BY SIZE

At first, springer spaniels and cocker spaniels were the same breed. Each **litter** was split by size. Over time, the larger dogs became springers. The smaller dogs became cockers.

Cocker spaniels (left) were bred to hunt small birds such as woodcocks and grouse.

Many springers still hunt today. They do other work, too. For example, some track people who are lost.

English springer spaniels have a better sense of smell than most dogs.

FAST FACT
Some springers are trained to smell **diseases**. They help doctors learn if people are sick.

CHAPTER 3

A SPRINGER'S LOOKS

Springers were bred to hunt all day. They are strong and energetic. Most springers weigh 40 to 50 pounds (18 to 23 kg).

English springer spaniels stand up to 20 inches (51 cm) tall at the shoulder.

Springers have long, silky ears. Each dog's coat has two layers. The undercoat is short and thick. The outer coat is longer. The layers keep springers warm and dry.

COAT COLORS

Springers can have several colors of fur. Many dogs are black and white. Others have a brownish color called liver. Tricolor coats are a mix of white, tan, and dark fur.

Some dogs have flecks on their coats. These spots are called ticking.

Dogs from the show line are sometimes called bench spaniels.

There are two **lines** of English springer spaniels. Dogs in the show line have longer fur and **feathering**. Field dogs are bred for hunting. They have shorter coats.

FAST FACT
Field spaniels tend to be smaller and faster than show dogs.

Springers can hunt in many types of weather.

CHAPTER 4

FAMILY DOGS

Springers are popular family pets. The dogs are smart and easy to train. They are also good with children.

Most springers want to please their owners.

Springers need lots of exercise. They should run and play at least an hour every day. Springers are strong swimmers and enjoy water.

DOG SPORTS

Many people train springers to compete in dog sports. In dock diving, dogs jump off a dock. They go as far as they can into the water. In agility, dogs run through **obstacle** courses.

At agility events, dogs often jump over hurdles.

Dogs may destroy things if they are alone for many hours.

Springers also need to be with people. If left alone too long, they can get bored or stressed. They might bark or chew things.

FAST FACT

Springers should be brushed once or twice a week. Their long ears need cleaning, too.

Long ears can trap dirt and germs. Cleaning them helps dogs stay healthy.

COMPREHENSION QUESTIONS

Write your answers on a separate piece of paper.

1. Write a few sentences explaining the main ideas of Chapter 2.

2. Would you like to own an English springer spaniel? Why or why not?

3. What were field springers bred to do?
    - A. be in shows
    - B. stay indoors
    - C. go hunting

4. Why would it be helpful for field springers to have shorter coats?
    - A. Shorter coats won't pick up as much dirt.
    - B. Shorter coats keep them from getting too cold.
    - C. Shorter coats help them move faster.

5. What does **split** mean in this book?

Each litter was split by size. Over time, the larger dogs became springers. The smaller dogs became cockers.

   A. tipped over
   B. kept together
   C. separated

6. What does **stressed** mean in this book?

Springers also need to be with people. If left alone too long, they can get bored or stressed. They might bark or chew things.

   A. upset or unhappy
   B. happy and calm
   C. needing alone time

Answer key on page 32.

GLOSSARY

breed

A specific type of dog with its own looks and abilities.

diseases

Sicknesses.

feathering

Long hair on a dog's ears, chest, legs, and belly.

illegal

Against the law.

lines

Different types of the same dog that are bred for different uses.

litter

A group of baby animals that are born at the same time.

obstacle

A thing that blocks the way.

retrieved

Picked up and brought back game that a hunter shot.

reward

Something given in return for good work.

TO LEARN MORE

BOOKS

Norton, Elisabeth. *Sniffer Dogs*. Mendota Heights, MN: Apex Editions, 2023.

Oachs, Emily Rose. *Sporting Dogs*. Minneapolis: Bellwether Media, 2021.

Pearson, Marie. *Dogs*. Mankato, MN: The Child's World, 2020.

ONLINE RESOURCES

Visit **www.apexeditions.com** to find links and resources related to this title.

ABOUT THE AUTHOR

Libby Wilson has loved books and reading her entire life. She enjoys researching and finding interesting facts to share with readers. Her favorite topics are nature, history, and inspirational people. For the past 11 years, Ms. Wilson has been owned by Molly, the world's sweetest golden retriever.

INDEX

A
agility, 24

B
birds, 10, 12
breed, 12–13

C
coat, 18, 20
cocker spaniel, 13

E
ears, 18, 27
Europe, 10
exercise, 24

F
field dogs, 20–21
fur, 18, 20

H
hunting, 10, 14, 16

P
police, 4, 7–8

R
retrieving, 10

S
show dogs, 20–21
sniffing, 8–9

ANSWER KEY:
1. Answers will vary; 2. Answers will vary; 3. C; 4. A; 5. C; 6. A